The
PSALMS SPEAK

George T. Peck

Pendle Hill Pamphlet 298

About the Author

This pamphlet grew out of a course taught at Pendle Hill in the autumn of 1989 by Mary Wood. As is usual in courses taken there, participants learn almost as much from fellow students as from the teacher. The author wishes to thank them all.

George and his wife, Annie, joined the Society of Friends by becoming members of the Stamford-Greenwich (CT) Meeting. On moving to Maine in 1981, they became founding members of the Brunswick Meeting and in 1986 spent a term as students at Pendle Hill. For the last twenty-five years, George has been active on the Board there and is author of several pamphlets, most recently *What is Quakerism?* (1988). Currently he is clerk of Quakers Uniting in Publications (QUIP), an international organization fostering outreach through the printed word.

Requests for permission to quote or translate should be addressed to Pendle Hill Publications, Wallingford, PA 19086.

Copyright © 1991 Pendle Hill
ISBN 0-87574-298-X
Library of Congress Card Number 91-062759
July 1991: 2,500

Certainly the psalms have spoken to many people in the twenty-four hundred years or so since they passed from oral to written tradition. The psalms still speak, but can we hear them? Our culture is decidedly not God-centered. Biblical illiteracy is commonplace in the contemporary world, especially among the educated. Whatever the mistrust or neglect, prayer and meditation can help a true seeker find a way back to the psalms, to history, and perhaps even to a spiritual home.

We readers mostly race through masses of printed material seeking the information needed for us to cope in our world. To read the psalms, one may try a more meditative reading, looking not for facts, but allowing the wisdom of the ages into our living experience. To allow this wisdom its space in our lives is not easy and takes time. Worshipful reading is a probing of the depths of consciousness best done in silence.

The psalms, for me, sing of the wisdom of lived experience. In these songs, the soul knows and is known by God, surviving the pain of suffering and the gloom of grief, risking honest hate and anger and making penance, seeking refuge from fears, learning to befriend the creation of which it is a part and finally coming to rest in the love of God, singing praises.

Intimacy with God

Psalm 139 conveys the intimacy of the psalmist with God with simplicity and majesty:

> O Lord, thou hast searched me, and known me.
> Thou knowest my downsitting and mine uprising, thou understandest my thought afar off.   Ps. 139:1-2

In approaching God, the psalmist sees God first in the distance, a transcendental unity overarching all the earth. Then

God comes closer:

> Thou compassest my path and my lying down,
> and art acquainted with all my ways.
> For there is not a word in my tongue,
> but, lo, O Lord, thou knowest it altogether.
> Thou has beset me behind and before,
> and laid thine hand upon me.   Ps. 139: 3-5

How does the psalmist, and how do we, react or respond to such closeness? Are we afraid, or trusting, or loving? If we are trusting, we may be just smug, whereas if we are fearful, we may be both unjust and ridden with guilt. The psalmist does not make it clear. "Such knowledge is too wonderful for me; it is high, I cannot attain unto it" (Ps. 139: 6).

Perhaps we are like the Rat and the Mole in The Wind in the Willows when they come into the presence of the "Piper at the gates of Dawn." The two animals have gone out on the river at first light to search for the baby otter and come on him asleep between the hooves of the great god Pan.

> Then suddenly the Mole felt a great Awe fall upon him, an awe that turned his muscles to water, bowed his head and rooted his feet to the ground. . . . He looked into the very eyes of the Friend and Helper, saw the backward sweep of the great horns gleaming in the growing daylight. . . .
>
> "Rat!" he found breath to whisper, shaking. "Are you afraid?"
>
> "Afraid," murmured the Rat, his eyes shining with unutterable love. "Afraid? of *Him*? O never, never! And yet-and yet-O Mole, I am afraid."
>
> And the two animals, crouching to the earth, bowed their heads and did worship.

Out of fear, it can be tempting to seek to escape from God. The psalmist considers this temptation to escape God's presence.

> Whither shall I go from thy spirit?
> or whither shall I flee from thy presence?
> If I ascend up into heaven, thou art there:
> if I make my bed in hell, behold, thou art there.
> If I take the wings of the morning,
> and dwell in the uttermost parts of the sea;
> Even there shall thy hand lead me,
> and thy right hand shall hold me.
> If I say, Surely the darkness shall cover me;
> even the night shall be light about me.
> Yea, the darkness hideth not from thee;
> but the night shineth as the day:
> the darkness and the light are both alike to thee.
> Ps. 139:7-12

How is it that the psalmist, and we too, find again and again and everywhere, the presence of God? Our life journeys are full of travel, changing our homes and occupations for most of us, and for all of us, facing new challenges and opportunities as we progress from babyhood to old age. But I have found that once having experienced that presence and its peace, it is not hard to set aside time each day for a moment of collection.

Even our bodies cannot escape the intimacy of God's knowing us.

> For thou hast possessed my reins:
> thou hast covered me in my mother's womb.
> I will praise thee; for I am fearfully and wonderfully made:
> marvellous are thy works;

and that my soul knoweth right well.
My substance was not hid from thee,
when I was made in secret,
and curiously wrought
in the lowest parts of the earth.
Thine eyes did see my substance, yet being unperfect;
and in thy book all my members were written,
which in continuance were fashioned,
when as yet there was none of them.   Ps. 139: 13-16

What does the word "reins" mean? Here is a Tudor word that has disappeared from modern parlance. It means "kidneys" and still the passage is obscure until we find out that in those days feelings were thought of as centering in the kidneys, just as we would say "gut feelings." A modern translation might be: "You have grabbed my guts," and it would capture the flavor of the original earthy Hebrew.

God knows our bodies by virtue of having created them from nothing. We accept readily the various mechanisms which science tells us mark the process of creation, but do we accept as clearly and as simply the universal life force behind all creation?

God knows us down to the bottom of our secret selves, even in the act of being conceived. Can any moment be more holy than that, more full of joy, more personal, more universal?

The psalmist goes even further in describing intimacy with God, when showing that before conception, and by implication after death, our existence is known in the mind of God. Many believers have been disturbed by the concept that an omniscient and omnipotent force determines all that we do. Arguments about pre-destination have raged for centuries, but I am content to rest in the faith that God knows and blesses.

If the sequence of the psalm represents an ever closer

approach to God, then the psalmist finds the climax in conscious thought.

> How precious also are thy thoughts unto me, O God!
> how great is the sum of them!
> If I should count them,
> they are more in number than the sand:
> when I awake, I am still with thee.   Ps. 139: 17-18

When in our thoughts we come close to God, we approach at the same time infinity, for note that God is as much present in our unconscious dream life as in conscious thought.

And so the psalm ends in a simple prayer:

> Search me, O God, and know my heart:
> try me, and know my thoughts:
> And see if there be any wicked way in me,
> and lead me in the way everlasting.   Ps. 139: 23-24

When reading the psalms meditatively, one way of knowing their wisdom is to surrender to the flow of the poetry. Ancient Hebrew poetics does not use a rhythmic structure like that of any Indo-European language, nor does it have any rhyme at all. Instead it often uses a form known as parallelism: the same idea is repeated in different words or one idea and its opposite are set forth repeatedly as seen in the first psalm, often thought of as a leitmotif for the whole collection.[1] This wedding of form and content in Hebrew poetics opens up challenging themes for understanding an intimate relationship with God:

> Blessed is the man that walketh not in the counsel of the ungodly,
> nor standeth in the way of sinners,
> nor sitteth in the seat of the scornful.
> But his delight is in the law of the Lord;

and in his law doth he meditate day and night.
And he shall be like a tree planted by the rivers of water,
that bringeth forth his fruit in his season;
his leaf also shall not wither,
and whatsoever he doeth shall prosper.
The ungodly are not so:
but are like the chaff which the wind driveth away.
Therefore, the ungodly shall not stand in the judgment,
not sinners in the congregation of the righteous.
For the Lord knoweth the way of the righteous:
but the way of the ungodly shall perish.   Ps. 1

Follow the godly worshipper as he or she walks, stands, sits, and finally comes to rejoice in the ordered harmony of creation. Note that the poetry is all in statements, full of verbs expressing inner action, rugged and simple with few modifying clauses. By contrast this modern commentary contains lots of adjectives and adverbs. The psalm has almost none at all, and herein lies its power.

Power also comes through the descriptive use of similes and metaphors. Here the worshipper in meditation can picture himself or herself to be like the tree in the psalm, drawing up divine energy from the moist earth mother and capturing the divine light of the sun father in its green leaves. Such a symbol can become a mantra to focus on unity with God.

The first psalm is divided precisely in two, the first three verses on the godly and the last three on the ungodly; each half has its simile. Over against the blessed serenity of God's unconditioned love is set the frantic pursuit of human desires. When unfulfilled, desire turns into frustration and anger, when fulfilled, into the melancholy of satiety. Both are fleeting and endlessly repeated-chaff for the winds of change.

In the second psalm, the battle between the godly and the

ungodly is carried to the cosmic level, where the Lord:

> shall speak unto them [the heathen] in his wrath,
> and vex them in his sore displeasure.
> . . .
> Thou shalt break them with a rod of iron;
> thou shalt dash them in pieces like a potter's vessel.
> Ps. 2:5,9

To many today such an angry, judgmental God seems incompatible with the biblical message of love, and so a stumbling block emerges for the understanding of the psalms.

Hatred

> Do not I hate them, O Lord, that hate thee?
> and am not I grieved with those
> that rise up against thee?
> I hate them with perfect hatred:
> I count them mine enemies. Ps. 139: 21-22

It would be surprising if poetry composed nearly three thousand years ago did not contain elements that I do not want to take into my consciousness for any purpose whatsoever—much less meditate on. This is true of the Hebrew psalms as it is of the roughly contemporary Greek Iliad. Rejecting, however, parts of the psalms while extolling others can lead to accusations of arrogance or worse. We are told that we should not select in Holy Writ only those passages which suit us. How then, can we understand these songs of hate?

The psalmists are at war. They are as embattled as ever Achilles and Hector were—passionately involved in the war between good and evil, vociferously and

and often self-righteously on God's side.

Psalm 137 contains a poisonous sting of hate, but not without a redemptive contradiction at its beginning:

> By the rivers of Babylon, there we sat down,
> yea, we wept, when we remembered Zion.
> We hanged our harps upon the willows in the midst thereof.
> For there they that carried us away captive required of us a song;
> and they that wasted us required of us mirth, saying,
> Sing us one of the songs of Zion.
> How shall we sing the Lord's song in a strange land?
> If I forget thee, O Jerusalem, let my right hand forget her cunning.   Ps. 137: 1-5

This scene has long been one of my favorites. I have shared the singers' dismay at the Babylonian Exile, their grief, their longing for home and their firm resolve to remain loyal to God. Then to be asked to sing! Only a singer can fully realize how terrible it is to sing when the breath is cut off by sobs. Then suddenly grief is turned into hatred:

> O daughter of Babylon, we art to be destroyed;
> happy shall he be, that rewardeth thee
> as thou hast served us.
> Happy shall he be, that taketh and dasheth
> thy little ones against the stones.   Ps. 137: 8-9

Described by a leading Jewish scholar as "a dreadful call for vengeance,"[2] these verses tell half the story of the West Bank; the other half being explained by the holy war preached by Mohammed (Koran 48,50), who personally led in the massacre of an entire Jewish settlement in 628. Vengeance is no special prerogative of Jews and Moslems. Think for example of St. Bernard's preaching of the crusade or watch on TV the sacking of abortion clinics by dedicated Christians. Whatever its origin, vengeance is abhorrent to me, but, according to the psalms, seems to be a real possibility once goodness is desired.

Does this mean that we should let evil win out over good? According to the bulk of Christian teaching, evil is not a power set over against God, as pictured for example in Job 1—but an aberration. Grief can give rise to hate out of a deep sense of injustice. But the honest acknowledgment of hate can lead back to grief and the capacity for forgiveness and reconciliation. Not only is God omnipotent and universal, but people are children of God, whether they admit it or not. Children make mistakes. They just seem to be evil when they are misbehaving out of ignorance or just contrariness.

A mother knows this. She comes into the room and finds her three-year-old attacking the new baby in a fit of sibling jealousy. Naturally she explodes. The child seeing this prop of existence changed into an ogre, bursts into tears of fear and guilt. Does Mother bash the child? Not if she is trying to follow the example of Jesus. She enfolds the child in a big cosy hug, as would an ape, and when things have calmed down a bit, she explains that this is not the way to behave.

To sum up, in the psalms, humanity at its fullest potential recognizes the aberration of evil, finds the song of redemption and sings it, braving the contradiction of singing in the face of captivity.

Suffering

Suffering is the alternative to hate once there is grief from injustice. Suffering can be the cauldron that stirs up hate or spews out cries of complaint to God. Laments or complaints form an important dimension in the psalms and scholars have classified about a third or more of the whole collection as laments. Only the theme of praise has an equal or greater prominence. Often it seems that the inner structure of many psalms is an uneven continuum between the two poles of lament and praise. The psalmist usually, but not always, starts with laments.

Laments can rarely be tied to a specific event. The reader never knows what sickness is referred to, nor can injustice or oppression be linked to any historical situation, except the Babylonian captivity in Psalm 137. The laments speak to me for the opposite reason; they portray the universal sufferings of humanity then and now and everywhere. I do not find that the inner landscape has changed much.

Of course, many of us do not want to admit suffering in any form; we strive to put a good face on things. "I'm fine." Perhaps this attitude is a survival from the last century, when suffering was commonly thought of as a reward for sin. If we were poor, it was our fault. If we were caught in a legal trap, we probably deserved it. If we were sick, it was because of harboring some evil thought or malpractice. On the other hand, if we were none of these, we were among the elect, and that was the place to be.

In this century a new way of looking at suffering has grown up; it is seen as a normal part of the human condition. Many today do not find it hard to admit to being angry, frustrated, afraid, lonely, depressed, oppressed, sad, or otherwise failing, though few like these conditions. We are learning to bring our weaknesses into the Light, to recognize them as our enemies when they can tempt us to hate, and then to discharge our negative feelings about them, allowing them to be embraced and strengthened in the Light.

A fellow Quaker told me that years ago, in his family, no

one was allowed to be angry, and it was only later that he learned that suppressing his feelings only distorted them and made them worse. A fellow student at the university taught me the same lesson. Bill was training to be a psychiatrist. He came around one day and asked me to come to the rifle range and shoot targets with him. And so we did for a whole winter. After a while Bill explained why he was doing this. He said that for both of us university life was full of tensions, highly competitive, and seemingly designed to reveal our shortcomings. As for him, he said that blasting away at a piece of paper made him feel good. I felt good, too. We were learning to dump our garbage of our personal conflicts, not in a public way which could lead to destructive aggressions, but privately and under controlled conditions.

Psychological therapy has widely and successfully applied the same principles. Carl F. Jung posited a "polarity inherent in all living things"—a psychic life that ranges between the poles of light and dark, male and female, good and bad, etc. His treatment led people to raise these stresses to the conscious level and then, when they had lost their sting, to cast them out. His goal, like that of the worshipper, was to reach the underlying unity behind the phenomena, as he put it, "to help patients find their structural base again." To him a creative spirit undergirds all the surface manifestations of the personality.

> For we are in the deepest sense the victims and the instruments of cosmogonic "love". . . . If he [man] possesses a grain of wisdom, he will lay down his arms and name the unknown by the more unknown . . . that is by the name of God. That is a confession of his subjection, his imperfection, his dependence, but at the same time a testimony to his freedom to choose between truth and error.[3]

The typical lament of the psalmist follows a parallel progression, i.e. from complaint (conscious expression of tensions), through petition (therapy), to praise (release). Psalm 13 is a classic example, devoting two verses to each stage.

> How long wilt though forget me, O Lord?
> for ever?
> how long wilt thou hide thy face from me?
> How long shall I take counsel in my soul,
> having sorrow in my heart daily?
> how long shall mine enemy be exalted over me?
> Ps. 13: 1-2

How long, how long, how long, how long? The four different but similar complaints form a fine example of repetitive parallelism. Like the psalmist, the worshipper can hug his or her own sorrow and rejection, can wallow in self-pity, construct secret scenarios of oppression and do it all in the most maudlin way imaginable. No stiff upper lip, for no one will hear it, except us and God, and we know about it already. Whatever the angst, we need only give it up to the Light until it begins to fade and we are freed to pray:

> Consider and hear me, O Lord my God:
> lighten mine eyes, lest I sleep the sleep of death;
> Lest mine enemy say, I have prevailed against him;
> and those that trouble me rejoice when I am moved.
> Ps. 13: 3-4

Here is a request for Light and for awareness. We need to be awake to alleviate sickness, perhaps, or to overcome depression. Light is needed to face oppression whether from society or family, "mine enemy," to see through the limitations imposed by economic circumstances and the greatest deprivation of all-death.

And so the psalmist ends with a declaration of trust and joy, true *tehillim*, the Hebrew word for praise.

> But I have trusted in thy mercy;
> my heart shall rejoice in thy salvation.
> I will sing unto the Lord,
> because he hath dealt bountifully with me.   Ps. 13: 5-6

Other verses of Psalm 22 deal with complaints of psychic and physical sickness.

> Be not far from me;
> for trouble is near;
> for there is none to help.
> Many bulls have compassed me:
> strong bulls of Bashan have beset me round.
> They gaped upon me with their mouths,
> as a ravening and a roaring lion.   Ps. 22: 11-13

The "bulls of Bashan" used to strike me as funny, because their slavering seemed to me as exotic as a lion's roaring. Both are very far from our suburbanized experience, but of course, the psalmist lived in a country that had both lions and bulls-and few fences. I notice that when walking in the country, I generally like to keep a fence between me and the bulls. These images can be metaphors of paranoid threat and can become very real to those who have experienced our modern surrealist poetry and art. Are not the figures of our feverish nightmares, as shown for example in Picasso's Guernica, very much like these ferocious animals?

Sickness can be physical as well as psychic:

> I am poured out like water,
> and all my bones are out of joint:
> my heart is like wax;

> it is melted in the midst of my bowels.
> My strength is dried up like a potsherd;
> and my tongue cleaveth to my jaws;
> and thou hast brought me into the dust of death.
> . . .
> I may tell all my bones:
> they look and stare upon me.   Ps. 22: 14, 15, 17

How we love to talk about our illnesses! and exaggerate them, as in "I am a worm." We revel in our feverishness, our emaciation that makes our bones stick out, our weaknesses, and our "being out of joint." It can be funny, too. Both the black humor and the wild complaint can lead us to impersonalize pain. As the pain ceases to dominate us, we can turn to God in thanks:

> For he hath not despised nor abhorred the affliction
> of the afflicted;
> neither hath he hid his face from him;
> but when he cried unto him, he heard.
> My praise shall be of thee
> in the great congregation:
> I will pay my vows before them that fear him.
>   Ps. 22: 24, 25

Grief

In the thought of Teilhard de Chardin, the greatest "diminishment" is death. When a dear one dies, one can do nothing about it. Few human beings can or wish to go through life without deep attachments to others, be they parents, children, friends, or perhaps dogs; and so when the separation of death occurs, few escape grief. Stop and think of your own experience of grief. When was it? Where?

For me it was picking up my dead baby from her crib forty-eight years ago. For me, Psalm 130 is the greatest lament, the unrestrained cry of grief.

> Out of the depths have I cried unto thee, O Lord.
> Lord, hear my voice:
> let thine ears be attentive to the voice
> of my supplications.   Ps. 130: 1-2

Out of the depths—*de profundis*. Grief seems to the psalmist, and to me, a kind of suffocation; time seems to stand still; deadness presses down on life. It is like being drowned. Or it is like being stuck in a filthy bog (Ps. 69: 2, 14). The way out is a desperate cry for help: *exaudi vocem meam*, hear my voice! How I would like to cry out as does the psalmist, but as an American, I find this hard. Our culture does not encourage the acceptance of grief and the full-throated roar of pain. I envy Filomena.

Filomena and Paolo lived in the "castello" which crowned the top of an Italian mountain town. Their place had once been the great kitchen of the castle, and I lived across the courtyard in a former guardroom. Paolo had been very ill, and one spring morning as I was walking across the courtyard with my daughter, a shriek burst from their place. I knew that Paolo had died and told my daughter to run and tell someone to come.

Paolo lay alone in the big bed. Filomena still screamed and began pulling at her hair. I held her fast, fearing she would hurt herself. Finally someone came to help hold her, and then more and more of the neighbors gathered. The screaming continued for hours, accompanied by a chorus of sympathy. During the afternoon the wailing became a rhythmical ululation that gradually subsided into a chant during the evening when the steady stream of mourners began to thin out.

A poet friend said that it reminded him of the choruses from Euripides' great pacifist drama, The Trojan Women, and another friend of an anthropological turn of mind added that such would not be the only survival from ancient Greece in Italian folklore.

The next day Filomena, dressed in the standard deep black of all Italian peasant women of her age, followed the bier for a kilometer out of town to the cemetery. Hundreds of black clothed friends were in the procession as the bell in the cathedral tolled once a minute all day, reminding all how grief drags down time.

The next day Filomena was herself again, perhaps a little bit hoarser than usual but okay. Paolo was not forgotten and would come up regularly in conversation, but Filomena's grief was purged.

Psalm 130 is also a penitential psalm:

> If thou, O Lord, shouldest mark iniquities,
> O Lord, who shall stand?
> But there is forgiveness with thee,
> that thou mayest be feared.   Ps. 130: 3-4

Here is an unconditional acceptance of sin. The psalmist makes no claim of self-justification and casts himself or herself on the love of a forgiving God. Trust has taken the place of argument.

> I wait for the Lord,
> my soul doth wait,
> and in his word do I hope.
> My soul waiteth for the Lord
> more than they that watch for the morning:
> I say, more than they that watch for the morning.
>   Ps. 130: 5-6

The psalmist is impatient, longing to escape from the weight of grief and the gloom of night. The King James Version repeats the verse to emphasize the eagerness. How often do we also lie awake at night yearning for the light of dawn to appear in the east!

Finally, while it may seem so, grief is never an isolated experience. Practically all know it and all can share in the rituals of death. In each individual grief, the community, "Israel," relives and releases its grief.

> Let Israel hope in the Lord:
> for with the Lord there is mercy,
> and with him is plenteous redemption.
> And he shall redeem Israel
> from all his iniquities.   Ps. 130: 7-8

Refuge

How wonderful it is to be able to seek and find refuge, safety, and comfort in God!

About a hundred years ago, it was almost fashionable to denigrate dependence on God as a cop-out, a dodging of burdens and problems by shifting them to imaginary shoulders. Nietzsche considered Christianity as a slave religion, and William Ernest Henley boasted of *his* soul as "unconquerable . . . whatever gods may be." But then I remember that Martin Luther never to my knowledge copped out on anything and yet wrote "A mighty fortress is our God/A bulwark never failing."

Luther may have drawn inspiration from Psalm 91:

> He that dwelleth in the secret place of the most High
> shall abide under the shadow of the Almighty.

> I will say of the Lord,
> He is my refuge and my fortress:
> my God; in him will I trust:
> Surely he shall deliver thee
> from the snare of the fowler,
> and from the noisome pestilence.
> He shall cover thee with his feathers,
> and under his wings shalt thou trust:
> his truth shall be thy shield and buckler.   Ps. 91: 1-4

Such a haven, a "shield and buckler," can be most desired in wartime. One of my teachers in school, a dear friend, told me that as a child he had gone to a great church in Hamburg, Germany, when the seemingly endless casualty lists from Verdun were being posted each day and few families went unscathed. Thousands sang "Ein feste Burg ist unser Gott/ein gute Werf und Waffen," and therein found refuge and strength. Another friend, this one a Quaker, told of coming to Pendle Hill in 1941 before entering on his alternative service as a conscientious objector and of finding in the godly community there a pool of peace in a raging world. As for me, I remember like yesterday the night in 1945 when I expected to be sent at dawn to the firing squad as a spy. Like the psalmist, I trusted in God to be delivered-by death or otherwise as God willed. It was important for me to learn the lesson that death on the earthly plane, no matter how massive or tragic, does not affect eternal life now or later.

The psalm continues with some very strong promises made to me and to you:

> Thou shalt not be afraid for the terror by night; nor for the arrow that flieth by day;
> Nor for the pestilence that walketh in darkness;
> nor for the destruction that wasteth at noonday.

> A thousand shall fall at thy side,
> and ten thousand at thy right hand;
> but it shall not come nigh thee.
> . . .
> Because thou hast made the Lord,
> which is my refuge,
> even the most High, thy habitation;
> There shall be no evil befall thee,
> neither shall any plague come nigh thy dwelling.
> For he shall give his angels charge over thee,
> to keep thee in all thy ways.
> They shall bear thee up in their hands,
> lest thou dash thy foot against a stone.
> Thou shalt tread upon the lion and adder:
> the young lion and dragon shalt thou trample under feet.
>
> Ps. 91: 5-7, 9-13

What assurances of protection! But do we actually believe them? Or are they just colorful, antique metaphors? There is indeed protection; as for me, war did not cut short forty-five more years. Pestilence sometimes spared a few. The great Sienese saints, Catherine and Bernardino, cared for sick and dying neighbors when the Black Death raged, and were spared. Father Damien served for years in the neglected leper colony on the island of Molokai before finally succumbing to the disease. Countless otherwise ordinary people, Christian Scientists, have led lives of quiet service in the midst of the paranoia arising from a succession of fashionable diseases. Yet few if any would lay claim to a faith that would protect us from all material diminishments. We buy insurance.

And pray:

> Because he hath set his love upon me,
> therefore will I deliver him:

> I will set him on high, because he hath known my name.
> He shall call upon me,
> and I will answer him:
> I will be with him in trouble;
> I will deliver him, and honour him.
> With long life will I satisfy him,
> and shew him my salvation.   Ps. 91: 14-16

Here is God's promise. The "I" of the psalm speaks directly to you and to me. In my experience it is God's greatest gift. God is always there to provide deliverance and honor. The paradox is that when we cry out in fear, God gives us courage.

I don't think the psalmist means the same thing by "long life" that I do. Most scholars believe that the psalmist hoped and expected to live on this material level to a ripe old age; to me that would be nice but irrelevant. The important promise is that life is not confined to any particular time and space, and so to me "long life" means eternal life.

The center of refuge and of greatest holiness was a special place in ancient Israel, Mt. Zion in Jerusalem. Every year the pious Jew hoped to make a pilgrimage there, and when the scribes were compiling the book of psalms, they indicated that psalms 120 through 134 were pilgrimage songs. (In the King James Version the ascription reads songs "of degrees," which may refer to climbing the steps of the Temple.) During the long centuries of the Diaspora, the faithful would say in hope, "Next year in Jerusalem." To many of them, as to many of us, Mt. Zion is a symbol: the "city of our God."

Psalm 121 is one such pilgrimage song:

> I will lift up mine eyes unto the hills,
> from whence cometh my help.
> My help cometh from the Lord,
> which made heaven and earth.

> He will not suffer thy foot to be moved:
> he that keepeth thee will not slumber.
> Behold, he that keepeth Israel
> shall neither slumber nor sleep.   Ps. 121: 1-4

Like most hikers, I "lift up mine eyes" to the goal of the walk. Climbing often seems a perfect paradigm of aspiration and reward. Although of late years the charms of attainment have faded, I still find peace and inspiration in the hills. The very monotony of walking irons out the stresses of life indoors and puts me again in the Presence. It is a joyful time; "the hills were joyful together" (Ps. 98:8). And so I know that my help cometh from the Lord.

Perhaps the pilgrims felt the same as they wandered through the barren hills of Judea and finally caught sight of the Temple of Solomon, where today shines the Dome of the Rock.

God shows untiring care for each individual and, by a natural transition, for the whole community or "Israel."

> The Lord is thy keeper:
> the Lord is thy shade upon thy right hand.
> The sun shall not smite thee by day,
> nor the moon by night.
> The Lord shall preserve thee from all evil:
> he shall preserve thy soul.
> The Lord shall preserve
> they going out and thy coming in
> from this time forth,
> and even for evermore.   Ps. 121:5-9

Of all these kinds of tender watchfulness, I cherish especially those that bless my "going out and coming in." All the gates of our experience, our beginnings and endings, our moments of passage, are holy.

Such a moment of holiness is dramatically captured in Psalm 24, which opens with an invocation to the Creator beginning "The earth is the Lord's and the fullness thereof . . . " (vv. 1-6). Then follows what some commentators have interpreted as a dialogue between the priests and a procession of pilgrims entering the Temple.

> Pilgrims: Lift up your hearts, O ye gates;
> and be ye lift up, ye everlasting doors;
> and the King of glory shall come in.
> Priests: Who is this King of glory?
> he Lord strong and mighty,
> the Lord mighty in battle.
> Pilgrims: Lift up your heads, O ye gates;
> even lift them up ye everlasting doors;
> and the King of glory shall come in.
> Priests: Who is this King of glory?
> he Lord of hosts,
> he is the King of glory. Selah.
> Ps. 24: 7-10

This vivid scene is from perhaps the oldest of all the psalms, for the Lord, "mighty in battle," is a theme that comes from the earliest Hebraic strata. Of Him sang Miriam when she celebrated the destruction of the Egyptians on the shores of the Red Sea (Ex. 15: 20-21), or again Deborah in her victory song after Israel's conquests in Palestine (Ju. 5). The community as a whole rejoices in God as a refuge.

And so can each one of us on our own, as shown in Psalm 46, which begins "God is our refuge, a very present help in trouble." The song ends on a note of quiet praise.

> Be still, and know that I am God:
> I will be exalted among the heathen,

I will be exalted in the earth.
The Lord of hosts is with us;
the God of Jacob is our refuge. Selah.
Ps. 46: 10-11

Befriending Creation

For anyone who carries a deep concern for heaven and earth, the psalms are an inspiration for meditation, a fresh liturgy, and a spiritual base for social concerns.

Here the proclamation of Psalm 19:

> The heavens declare the glory of God;
> and the firmament sheweth his handywork. Day unto day uttereth speech,
> and night unto night sheweth knowledge.
> There is no speech nor language,
> where their voice is not heard.
> Their line is gone out through all the earth,
> and their words to the end of the world.
> In them hath he set a tabernacle for the sun,
> Which is as a bridegroom coming out of his chamber,
> and rejoiceth as a strong man to run a race.
> His going forth is from the end of the heaven,
> and his circuit to the ends of it:
> and there is nothing hid from the heat thereof.
> Ps. 19: 1-6

Using the metaphor of speech, the psalmist celebrates the rationality and interrelatedness of all phenomena—what environmentalists often think of as the "seamless web of creation," no one thread of which may be disturbed without affecting all the others. What a blessing it is to take this vision into inner experience!

One sparkling night as a schoolboy, I was coming back from the movies and lay down in the middle of the football field. I looked up at the stars and the milky way, shining with incredible clarity. To me they declared the glory of God and so did the black spaces in between, for I could barely grasp their immensity. What if I were to fall off my little planet? I dug my fingers into the turf of dear mother earth and then laughed at myself and never admitted to any one my moment of worship.

Often the stars would speak to me and so I came to know their language. First, this language was the wordless assurance of regularity, order, and harmony. Then I began to explore some of the regularities and gave them names so as to be friendly with them, as Adam did with the animals: the Giant Hunter, his Big Dog, the great square of the Flying Horse, the Twins, the Bull, and the dancing Pleiades. Virgil taught me to look for the Pleiades when the rains of autumn come and they rise just before dawn. When out in the woods, I would wait for the coming of the sun. What power, joy, and life he brought! Like a bridegroom.

So this cosmos was home to me and in it I felt the presence of God, often unconsciously. Then I went to New Zealand, where I found that the Hunter just made it over the northern horizon. The sun was always in the north so that when I was walking west, it felt like going east. Only then did I understand how profoundly the heavens embraced my life and realize that I was truly away from home.

When the astronauts took the first pictures of the Blue Planet from outer space, all could see the beauty and fragility of our ecosystem. Many environmentalists in their passion to protect nature have turned to the powerful nature mythologies of non-European peoples. While they draw strength from these sources, some have abandoned their own traditions, accusing the "hierarchical nature of Judeo-Christian theology, which removes human beings from the natural world and places them in control of it. . . . We need to see ourselves, humbly, as part of the earth, going beyond such concepts as 'stewardship.'"[4]

Such an interpretation is easily understandable, since some professed Christians have been wholesale exploiters of natural resources to satisfy human need and greed. Christianity is the religion of Europe, whose peoples, animals, plants, insects, and germs overran much of the world and altered if not obliterated non-European ecologies.[5] When the pathogens they brought with them decimated the "natives," many Christian Europeans believed that God had brought pestilence so that the land would be empty and so open for settlement.

But does scripture teach that a true steward could be an exploiter? I don't think so. Let us return to Psalm 19:

> The law of the Lord is perfect, converting the soul:
> the testimony of the Lord is sure, making wise the simple.
> The statutes of the Lord are right, rejoicing the heart:
> the commandment of the Lord is pure, enlightening the eyes.
> The fear of the Lord is clean, and enduring forever:
> the judgments of the Lord are true and righteous altogether.
> More to be desired are they than gold,
> yea, than much fine gold:
> sweeter also than honey and the honeycomb.
> Ps. 19: 7-10

The psalmist is talking about what we would call natural law, both in the ecological and the social dimension. Law is thus a declaration of harmony and so of God in all creation.

It does not seem accidental that Newton was describing expectable regularities in the physical world at the same time that Hobbs and Grotius were doing the same for the world of human relations. Their mindset laid the basis for the Enlightenment and found expression in the classical balance of the art of Addison, Watteau, and Haydn.

But we often depart from the enjoyment of serenity and peace.

> Who can understand his errors?
> cleanse thou me from secret faults.
> Keep back thy servant also from presumptuous sins;
> let them not have dominion over me:
> then shall I be upright,
> and I shall be innocent from the great transgression.
>
> Ps. 19: 12-13

It seems to me that lapses from grace are often unintentional, although I can think of few that were purposefully malicious. For example, the Maoris didn't know that when they brought their dogs and rats to New Zealand, they were dooming to extinction moas and most of the phyla of flightless birds. In a like fashion, we can look back at the settlement of continents by Europeans and know that they were very bad stewards indeed, mostly because they did not foresee the end results of their actions. Will future generations look back on us, developers and environmentalists alike, with the same repugnance?

We can join humbly in the prayer of the psalmist.

> Let the words of my mouth,
> and the meditation of my heart,
> be acceptable in thy sight,
> O Lord, my strength and my redeemer.   Ps. 19: 14

Of similar significance to environmentalists is Psalm 104,

which contains extended reflections on the first and second chapters of Genesis. The creation story is among the most controversial passages in the whole Bible, an inadvertent tribute to its continuing relevance. Is it history or metaphor? Does or should Adam rule all nature? Is Eve an afterthought? These and other questions can lead to heated debates. But since argument stops meditation, let us turn to the psalm and draw from it what is relevant.

> Bless the Lord, O my soul.
> O Lord my God, thou art very great;
> thou art clothed with honour and majesty.
> Who coverest thyself with light as with a garment:
> who stretchest out the heavens like a curtain:
> Who layeth the beams of his chambers in the waters:
> who maketh the clouds his chariot:
> who walketh upon the wings of the wind.
>
> Ps. 104: 1-3

The first creation is the light. How differently from the psalmist do we look at light today. We imagine the blinding flash of the big bang, try to understand the complexities of sub-atomic physics, and watch computer simulations on the TV. By contrast the psalmist, calling on the accepted evolutionary theory of his time, describes divine spiritual motion. God as creator was and is still a central religious experience, but God's clothes have changed. The psalmist speaks of garments, curtains, and chambers; God is pictured in human form. Does this make God small? No, only that human shapes are ones we can understand with our limited vision. God's form is cosmic—"he that sitteth upon the circle of the earth" (Is. 40: 21-31).

Often our view of creativity is human-oriented, as when we speak of a "creative personality," or "creative art," or the "creative urge." To one who worships in the presence of the One Creator, human creativity is nothing but a pale deeply treasured reflection of the divine. Medieval artists rarely signed their works, for to do so would be presumptuous, would detract from God.

The psalmist centers on God:

> Who laid the foundations of the earth,
> that it should not be removed forever.
> Thou coveredst it with the deep as with a garment:
> the waters stood above the mountains.
> At thy rebuke they fled;
> at the voice of thy thunder they hasted away.
> They go up by the mountains;
> they go down by the valleys
> unto the place which thou hast founded for them.
> Thou hast set a bound that they may not pass over;
> that they turn not again to cover the earth.   Ps. 104: 5-9

To a people who lived mostly out of doors in a rough, mountainous, and semi-arid country, floods, whirlwinds, thunderstorms, and eruptions were "acts of God" of a strongly intimate nature. The great geological forces shape the earth, and specifically in the Great Rift valley, where the effects of continental drift and volcanic action are much in evidence. In Hawaii, another geologically young region, natives worship the creator God in the form of the goddess Pele, and some have objected to the building of a geothermal plant on the slopes of a volcano as a violation of her home. Should we Christians be less respectful and less humble in the presence of creative evolution?

The psalmist continues to reflect on creation:

> He sendeth the springs into the valleys,

> which run among the hills.
> They give drink to every beast of the field:
> the wild asses quench their thirst.
> By them shall the fowls of the heaven have their habitation,
> which sing among the branches.
> He watereth the hills from his chambers:
> the earth is satisfied with the fruit of thy works.
> He causeth the grass to grow for the cattle,
> and herb for the service of man:
> that he may bring forth food out of the earth;
> and wine that maketh glad the heart of man, and oil to make his face to shine, and bread which strengtheneth man's heart.
> The trees of the Lord are full of sap;
> the cedars Of Lebanon, which he hath planted;
> Where the birds make their nests:
> as for the stork, the fir trees are her house.
> The high hills are a refuge for the wild goats;
> and the rocks for the conies.   Ps. 104: 10-18

Earlier commentators attributed the prominent position of water in the psalmist's world to the dryness of Palestine, but nowadays we residents of wet climates have learned to prize water just as highly. It's what makes us call our world the Blue Planet, now that we can see it from outer space. So many of our waters are polluted that we yearn for what St. Francis called "sister water which is very useful, humble, precious, and chaste." We join with the little poor man of Assisi in admiring the beauty and freedom of birds. Like the psalmist, we are inclined to be most grateful for the gifts which the Creator gives us from our fields: food, wine, and bread. No longer do our faces shine with olive oil, since the invention of soap led to a different type of cosmetics.

This passage is reminiscent of Hesiod's <u>Work and Days</u> of about the same period. The Greek, the Jew, and the modern environmentalist rejoice in unity with nature:

> He appointed the moon for seasons:
> the sun knoweth his going down.
> Thou makest darkness, and it is night:
> wherein all the beasts of the forest do creep forth.
> The young lions roar after their prey,
> and seek their meat from God.
> The sun ariseth,
> they gather themselves together,
> and lay them down in their dens.
> Man goeth forth unto his work
> and to his labor until the evening.   Ps. 104: 19-23

As diurnal animals, we and the psalmist tend to notice things that impact on us, such as days and nights. We divide the hours into minutes and seconds and know that one second equals one heartbeat. It is easy to be self-centered. Not often do we think of the fact that birds, which have about six heartbeats a second, must live six times faster.

It is also easy to picture people as the top of the hierarchy of nature and to conclude that we dominate nature—giving names to all other creatures, as did Adam (Gen. 2: 19-20). To many, Adam seems a male chauvinist, but the dominance of the human species, metaphorically Adam, is an established fact—now even more than then. Not only are we able to think of other creatures objectively and thus name them, but we are fully able to manipulate most others, including pathogens. It is the unparalleled success of humanity, especially in this century, which presents the main threat to the balance of nature.

Our prominence also means that we are the most dangerous

of species and have frequently torn the seamless web of creation. The message of this psalm, according to C.S. Lewis, is that our prominence lays on us a greater responsibility.[6] Lewis points out that all creatures, whether useful or harmful to people, are on the same level: grass, trees, birds, goats, conies as well as lions and the "great beasts" of the sea. These last are not only of no apparent use to people but downright dangerous. Modern ecology tries to teach man, the greatest predator, respect for other predators. We are united in being children of God:

> O Lord, how manifold are thy works!
> in wisdom hast thou made them all:
> the earth is full of thy riches.
>
> . . .
>
> These wait all upon thee;
> that thou mayest give them their meat in due season.
> That thou givest them they gather:
> thou openest thine hand,
> they are filled with good.
> Thou hidest thy face,
> they are troubled:
> thou takest away their breath,
> they die, and return to their dust.   Ps. 104: 24, 27-29

God provides for all of us, handing out the food to sustain the life he gives us. So we thank God when we sit down at our dinner tables and again when we fill the bird feeders.

We end our meditation with praise and thanks:

> The glory of the Lord shall endure for ever:
> the Lord shall rejoice in his works.
> He looketh at the earth, and it trembleth:
> he toucheth the hills, and they smoke.

> I will sing unto the Lord as long as I live:
> I will sing praise to my God while I have my being.
> My meditation of him shall be sweet:
> I will be glad in the Lord.   Ps. 104: 31-34

Praise

Praise is the most frequent and strongest theme in the psalms. It is the ultimate polarity of worship. The soul survives the pain of suffering and the gloom of grief, risks hate, makes penance, seeks refuge from fears, learns to befriend nature and finally comes to rest in the love of God, singing praises. Perhaps some such pattern was in the minds of the scribes who first set the psalms in order, for they placed five psalms of praise at the end of the whole collection.

My experience is that this journey is not a linear one from point A to point B. One does not, like Christian in Bunyan's Pilgrim's Progress, have to slog though all the stages of human suffering and sin in order to earn the blessing of God's love. Rather, at some one point in time and space, the free gift of God's grace comes into the ken of conscious awareness-unexpected, unplanned, and unsought. God's loves comes quite beyond human will and thinking, but often available to human feeling.

Once this joy has been experienced, then it is indeed sought again often in the silence of worship. The problem is that we forget. We succumb to the temptation to believe in a reality other than God, be it in the form of external circumstances, the power of sickness, the specter of poverty, or the fear of the death of the body. These daily trials can dislodge us from our center of light, and we feel the need to remember the unconditional love of God.

The psalms of love and trust can be reminders. Most often psalmists express God's love in some particular manifestation, such as God's "name." "law," or "house." God is praised for "mercies," "lovingkindness," and "goodness,"-forms that stress transcendence. But also the psalmists' experience of intimacy with God points to the God within and looks forward to the absolute and unlimited love of God.

Twenty centuries of Christian devotion have also fed my meditations. The burning *affectus* which Augustine or Hippo expressed in his remorselessly honest and revealing Confessions, lived on in the dedication of countless worshippers to God. The humble Francis made God's love his daily companion, and his followers have lived in his testimony in, for example, bringing shelter and nurture to the poor. Early Friends were often "tendered" in the love of God, and today Quakers still answer the call of compassion when they hear it.

Such tenderness flows from the yearning of the individual soul for God. It is the wellspring of Bonaventure's Journey of the Mind into God. In notable contrast to the Buddhist tradition, Jewish and Christian devotion is full of desire.

> As the hart panteth after the water brooks,
> so panteth my soul after thee, O God.
> My soul thirsteth for God, for the living God:
> when shall I come and appear before God?
> My tears have been my meat day and night,
> while they continually say unto me,
> Where is thy God?   Ps. 42: 1-3

One of the rewards of love is joy. It is not possible to give out love or joy and have less, for these are gifts that feed upon themselves and grow every stronger. Psalm 100 carries the ascription "a song of praise:"

> Make a joyful noise unto the Lord,
> all ye lands.
> Serve the Lord with gladness:
> come before his presence with singing.
> Know ye that the Lord he is God:
> it is he that hath made us, and not we ourselves;
> we are his people,
> and the sheep of his pasture.
> Enter into his gates with thanksgiving,
> and into his courts with praise:
> be thankful unto him, and bless his name.
> For the Lord is good;
> his mercy is everlasting;
> and his truth endureth to all generations.   Ps. 100

It seems fitting that these meditations of mine which started with the theme of intimacy with God should end with the declaration of total trust expressed in Psalm 23. Here is no striving, no petition, but only the simple and direct statement of fact. The psalmist does not need to strain toward a future goal, but just rests in the assurance of a loving presence right now. Perhaps the reason that this is the best known and most beloved of all the psalms arises from its existential reality. Its truth is as clear as a multiplication table.

> The Lord is my shepherd;
> I shall not want.
> He maketh me to lie down in green pastures:
> he leadeth me beside the still waters.
> He restoreth my soul:
> he leadeth me in the paths of righteousness
> for his name's sake.   Ps. 23: 1-3

But stop and re-read. These verses are as familiar as the

Mona Lisa; thus, we may be tempted to slide over them as though they were merely a well-worn formula, a trite chromo on the classroom wall. Let us savor them for they are full of surprises.

The Lord a shepherd? But is this not to us a far-fetched metaphor? In my travels around this country, I do not recall ever having met a shepherd, although I have seen them from afar in the great Wyoming spaces. Yet this symbol conveys caring simply and beautifully.

Because of this caring love, I shall never go hungry or thirsty. What a statement! Pure pie in the sky. That is not the reason most of us think we shall not want. Most of us usually think: "I have a job and savings; I shall not want." We spend an inordinate amount of time trying to keep it that way. Eventually I might reach the conviction of the psalmist that a just God will reward me, and at the end of a good work day rest in the grass by a quiet pond.

But is society always just and does God through society always provide? Of course not. Want is everywhere to be found, whether in the crude shelters of the homeless in our cities to the distant Sahel. I find poverty an intolerable aberration, hoping always to see it disappear. May I, and others, sometime reach the faith that the psalmist states as a fact and so find my soul restored.

Now the psalmist shifts gears from speaking of God as "he" to the more direct and personal "thou:"

> Yea, though I walk through
> the valley of the shadow of death,
> I will fear no evil:
> for thou art with me;
> thy rod and thy staff they comfort me.   Ps. 23: 4

The psalm expands from the minor to the major key as it

makes the affirmation about death. Many times that affirmation has brought solace to the survivors at a funeral service. I am grateful that I was born before parents were taught to pretend in front of the children that death doesn't exist. My mother had me learn the old children's prayer: "Now I lay me down to sleep/I pray the Lord my soul to keep/If I should die before I wake/I pray the Lord my soul to take." And I rested in his protection and peace. I always thought of God as "he," but the shining angel at the end of the bed, who kept off the goblins of the dark corners, was "she."

God is our host and hostess and lays the table for friendship.

> Thou preparest a table before me
> in the presence of mine enemies:
> thou anointest my head with oil;
> my cup runneth over.   Ps. 23: 5

While we may start out the dinner as enemies or perhaps just as strangers, we become friends, children of God in common by the end of the main course. And there is plenty for all, for "my cup runneth over." And so the psalm ends as we are all gathered in our cosmic home.

> Surely goodness and mercy shall follow me
> all the days of my life:
> and I will dwell in the house of the Lord forever.
> Amen.   Ps. 23: 6

Notes

1. Samuel Sandmel, The Enjoyment of Scripture (New York, 1972) pp. 8-13, 188-195. John B. Gabel and Charles B. Wheeler, The Bible as Literature 2nd ed.; (New York, 1990) chapter 14. Walter Brueggemann, Praying the Psalms (Philadelphia, 1986). Arthur Wieser, The Psalms (Philadelphia, 1962). Claus Westermann, The Living Psalms (Grand Rapids, 1969).

2. Sandmel, The Enjoyment of Scripture, p. 206.

3. C.F. Jung, Memories, Dreams, Reflections (New York, 1961), p. 354.

4. "Befriending Creation," Friends in Unity with Nature, Vol. 3, No. 6 (Feb. 1990).

5. Alfred W. Crosby, Ecological Emperialism, the Biological Expansion of Europe (Cambridge, 1986).

6. C.S. Lewis, Reflections on the Psalms (New York, 1958), pp. 77-85.

Pendle Hill

PENDLE HILL is a residential study center and a retreat and conference center as well as the publisher of Pendle Hill books and pamphlets. It is a center for the nurture of religious life and an adult school for intensive study in those fields which help unfold the meaning of life. At Pendle Hill education is thought of in its broadest sense—the transforming of persons and society.

Pendle Hill offers a three term **residential program** from October to June. 35 to 40 persons, ranging in age from 19 to 75, enroll as students for one or more terms, joining the resident staff and families. About half the community are Friends. Among the rest a wide variety of faiths, philosophies, and cultural backgrounds is represented. Students pursue interests and concerns through study, reading, writing, meditation, dialogue, and creative projects. Each morning residents gather in **meeting for worship,** held after the manner of Friends. Pendle Hill offers five or six **courses** in the area of Quakerism, Bible, religious thought, peace and social concerns, literature and the arts, and crafts. Every student participates in the **work program,** helping with the upkeep of house and grounds and with food preparation and meal clean-up.

Admission to Pendle Hill is based upon the applicant's commitment to learning, openness to exploring religious reality, and readiness to take a responsible part in the common life of Pendle Hill. Limited **financial aid** is available for applicants unable to pay the full fees.

Pendle Hill also offers a full program of short term events through its **Extension Program:** weekend conferences and retreats; summer workshops, conferences, and retreats; a series of Monday Evening Lectures; weekly extension courses for persons not living at Pendle Hill. Persons wishing a short term experience in the resident community may also apply to be **sojourners** during most of the year.

Further details on dates and fees for all programs are available from **Pendle Hill, Wallingford, PA 19086. 215-566-4507.**